BBC

Gardeners' World

POCKET

PATIO PLANTS

Andi Clevely

BBC Books

Author Biography

Andi Clevely has been a working gardener for nearly thirty years. He began his career in Leeds City Council central nurseries and since then has worked in many gardens around the country, including Windsor Great Park. He is now responsible for a country estate and large garden in Stratford-on-Avon where he lives with his family. Andi has written a number of gardening books and presents a weekly gardening programme.

Acknowledgements

The publishers would like to thank Secretts Garden Centre, Godalming, Surrey, and The Royal Horticultural Society Gardens, Wisley, Surrey, for their assistance with the photography. Photographs by Jo Whitworth © BBC except the following pages: Garden Picture Library 6 (Vaughan Fleming), 21, 41 (Howard Rice), 45, 75 (John Glover), 73 (Brian Carter); Photos Horticultural 12, 19, 20, 49, 51, 55, 70, 80; Harry Smith Collection 66.

Published by BBC Books, an imprint of BBC Worldwide Limited,
Woodlands, 80 Wood Lane, London W12 0TT

First published 1998
© BBC Worldwide Limited 1998
The moral right of the author has been asserted

ISBN 0 563 38420 4

Artwork by Pond and Giles

Set in Futura

Printed and bound in Belgium by Proost NV
Colour separations by Radstock Reproductions Limited, Midsomer Norton, Avon
Cover printed in Belgium by Proost NV

Planning the Patio Garden

🌿 **Bold** denotes
evergreen plants.

INTRODUCTION

Patio gardening is the term widely used to describe growing plants outdoors in containers, on balconies, terraces and paved areas. It is not a poor relation of open-ground gardening, and in fact offers several advantages: plants are easier to reach in pots and are less prone to pest attacks, while containers can be moved around when their display is over or simply to change an arrangement. Above all, the range of plants is increased because you can grow varieties that are tender or not suited to your garden soil.

Choosing containers

Test their weight, especially if you are gardening on a balcony or rooftop, or might need to move a heavy plant. Tall narrow pots may topple easily in exposed positions. A squat one is more stable but may need extra watering if it is shallow.

Although an alpine sink can be only 10cm (4in) deep, most plants need 20cm (8in) for healthy root growth, and larger perennials and shrubs require at least 30cm (12in). Have a range of pot sizes, partly to match different plant types and growth rates, and also because as plants develop you will need to move them to larger containers. More water and nutrients will be available in large pots.

Materials vary widely and are largely a matter of personal preference; if plants have special needs this is mentioned in the text. Check that containers are frost-proof if they are to stand outside all year, and, if possible, raise them off the ground on blocks or short legs to aid drainage. Window-boxes and hanging baskets should be securely fixed for safety.

Composts for containers

Don't be tempted to economize by using garden soil – except perhaps for shrubs in large containers, where equal amounts of very good quality soil and potting compost can be mixed together – as this can lead to problems with drainage. Avoid these by using a potting compost.

Soil- or loam-based mixtures are heavy. They make pots more stable and help to support tall plants, but full containers may be difficult to move. Soil-less composts, usually sold as multi-purpose mixtures, are lighter and cleaner, although they can dry out quickly and then prove difficult to water. The preferred type is mentioned in each entry. A proportion of sharp sand or grit, about 25 per cent, can be added for species needing enhanced drainage.

Planting in containers

Thoroughly clean out used containers before refilling them, and soak new clay pots overnight. All containers for outdoor use must have drainage holes in the base. Set large units in position before filling.

- Containers with numerous small holes do not usually need a drainage layer if you are using soil-less compost. Otherwise, protect the holes with broken tiles or pieces of clay pot; in large containers cover these crocks with gravel, small stones or broken polystyrene packaging, up to 5cm (2in) deep where extra drainage is recommended.

- Water the plants and leave them to drain for an hour or two. Fill the container about two-thirds full of compost, and press it down gently or leave it to settle for a day or two; the contents of old grow-bags can be used in the lower part to reduce the volume of fresh compost needed.

- Arrange plants to your satisfaction on the surface, a little closer than you would in the open garden, and then remove them from their pots.

- Starting with the largest, dig out a hole large enough to take the roots comfortably, and with the top of the rootball just below the surface of the surrounding soil. Firm into position, continue planting, and finish with a level surface 2.5–5cm (1–2in) below the rim. Water in gently.

- For single plants, choose a container 5–8cm (2–3in) wider than the one in which it is growing. Cover the drainage hole with crocks and a layer of compost. Tap the plant from its pot and place in the centre of the layer of compost. Fill the surrounding space with compost and firm or tap into place. Water thoroughly.

Care

Watering: Check containers regularly, every day in hot or windy conditions when pots dry quickly; even after rain the compost may remain dry in sheltered positions. Small pots and fully exposed containers such as hanging baskets dry faster than tubs with a large volume of compost. A dry surface may indicate that watering is needed, but test by pushing your finger about 2.5cm (1in) into the compost. Plants with flagging leaves are seriously demanding water. When watering, always fill containers gently to the brim once or twice, leaving them to drain in between.

If pots are very dry and the water runs straight through, stand them in a deep bowl of water for a few hours.

Feeding: Composts normally contain enough nutrients for at least 6 weeks' growth; after this, especially when plants are in flower, supplementary feeding

becomes necessary, usually until the end of the growing season – see individual entries for recommended frequencies. Use a balanced liquid fertilizer, diluted according to instructions, and water on the compost when it is moist.

Slow-release fertilizers, compressed into pellets or sticks, are a useful alternative for some plants and supply enough food for several months.

Winter care: Tender plants and small pots should be moved indoors or to a sheltered frost-free position in autumn. Hardy plants are normally safe in large containers, but can be covered with layers of horticultural fleece or sacking; insulate the pots with straw held in place with sacking, or several thicknesses of bubble plastic. Small pots may be plunged up to the rim and close together in an unplanted tub or half-barrel to protect their roots from freezing.

Repotting: The compost in which permanent plants are growing usually needs annual refreshment. Small plants can be transferred to the next size pot. Alternatively, repot in the same size container: remove the plant, tease away some of the old compost with a hand-fork or seed label, and trim the roots by up to 25 per cent; then pot up in the usual way. Plants that are too large to be repotted are top-dressed: scrape away the top 5–8cm (2–3in) of old compost and replace this with a fresh layer.

Propagation: Annuals are raised from seeds sown at the times specified; perennials are usually propagated by division or from cuttings, although some may be grown from seed. Depending on the space available under glass, you can take cuttings from tender perennials in summer or autumn and then discard the old plants, or overwinter the plants to provide cuttings in spring.

ACER PALMATUM 'DISSECTUM ATROPURPUREUM'

The neat foliage of these classic shrubs is decorative all season, but in autumn the leaves catch fire with colour and flame in gorgeous shades of bronze, purple, scarlet and ruby. Give one pride of place in a special container, and complete the composition by underplanting it with dwarf winter or early spring bulbs.

Plant type:	Hardy perennial deciduous shrub or small tree.
Season:	Foliage spring to mid-autumn; vivid late colours.
Height:	Up to 2.4m (8ft).
Spread:	1.8–2.4m (6–8ft).
Positioning:	Light or semi-shade, sheltered from cold winds and sun scorch. As a specimen in a tub or half-barrel.
Care:	Plant in autumn or spring in soil-based compost. Always keep moist but avoid over-watering. Shelter from late spring frosts or protect with fleece. Top-dress in spring, mulch with well-rotted manure or composted bark. Watch out for aphids on young shoots. Repot every 4–5 years.
Propagation:	May be raised from seeds sown outdoors in autumn.
Recommended:	'Crimson Queen', 'Osakazuki', 'Garnet', 'Sango-kaku' (syn. 'Senkaki'), finely cut var. *dissectum*.
Useful tip:	Buy plants in autumn to judge the best coloured forms.

Agapanthus African Lily

Plant type: Hardy herbaceous perennial; fleshy roots.

Season: Flowers mid-summer to early autumn.

Height: 75cm (30in).

Spread: 38–45cm (15–18in).

Positioning: Full sun, best against a warm wall. Singly or in groups of 3 in large pots or tubs.

Care: Plant in spring: bury crowns 5cm (2in) deep in soil-based compost with extra grit around their tips. Water freely when dry; liquid feed once or twice in mid-summer. Cut stems down after flowering unless seeds are to be saved. Do not disturb roots until over-crowding indicates division is necessary. Top-dress in spring.

Propagation: Divide roots in spring; sow seeds in a frame in spring.

Recommended: *A. campanulatus* and var. *albidus*, 'Isis', 'Profusion', ssp. *patens*; also named hybrids like 'Ben Hope', 'Headbourne Hybrids', 'Loch Hope'.

Useful tip: Plants are evergreen if kept above 0°C (32°F) in a cool conservatory.

AGAPANTHUS 'BEN HOPE'

The tall stately flowers of Agapanthus are typically blue although white and mauve varieties are also available. Despite a reputation for being tender and needing cool greenhouse protection, its many hybrids survive normal winters outdoors, especially in the shelter of a warm wall. Sowing home-saved seed often yields a mixed bag of exciting shades.

Amaranthus caudatus Love-Lies-Bleeding

AMARANTHUS CAUDATUS

Amaranthus has been a favourite summer flower since the 16th century. When well-grown, with plenty of water in a dry season, its conspicuous trailing ropes of tiny bright flowers can reach 45cm (18in) long, and its large, fresh green leaves turn a rich shade of coppery orange or crimson in autumn, complementing its bright red stems.

Plant type:	Half-hardy annual summer bedding plant.
Season:	Flowers early summer to early autumn; coloured foliage all season.
Height:	30cm–1.2m (1–4ft).
Spread:	30–60cm (1–2ft).
Positioning:	Full sun. 3 in a 30cm (12in) pot or singly as a centrepiece in a large mixed container.
Care:	Plant after the last frosts in multi-purpose compost. Water in thoroughly; keep moist all season. In windy sites support stems with twiggy sticks. Liquid feed once or twice in mid-summer with high-potash fertilizer. Discard old plants.
Propagation:	Sow under glass at 21°C (70°F) in early spring; move seedlings to small pots.
Recommended:	Basic species and green 'Viridis'; dwarf 'Green Thumb'; also variegated *A. tricolor* (Joseph's Coat), var. *splendens* (crimson).
Useful tip:	*A. tricolor* forms are are best grown in a sheltered spot or under glass.

Anemone blanda Windflower

Plant type: Hardy herbaceous perennial; rhizomatous roots.

Season: Flowers late winter to mid-spring.

Height: 10cm (4in).

Spread: 5–10cm (2–4in).

Positioning: Full sun or semi-shade. 5cm (2in) apart in groups in pots and troughs, underplanted in larger containers.

Care: Plant in early to mid-autumn, 5–8cm (2–3in) deep, in multi-purpose compost. After flowering leave underplanted tubers to die down naturally; plant those in small pots in the open garden or give a liquid feed every 7–10 days until leaves fade.

Propagation: Divide dense clumps in late summer; replant immediately.

Recommended: Basic species and named selections like 'Charmer', 'Radar', var. *rosea*, 'White Splendour'.

Useful tip: The florist's anemones 'De Caen' and 'St Brigid' thrive in pots, for a single flowering season or as long-term perennials.

ANEMONE BLANDA

The pretty daisy-like flowers seem to open at the slightest touch of late winter and spring sunshine and have a unique charm. They appear in a fine range of colours, from white to red and blue. Plant them generously, on their own or beneath larger perennials and shrubs.

Antirrhinum majus Snapdragon

ANTIRRHINUM MAJUS

A popular old-fashioned summer flower, with distinctive fragrant blooms. Each has a prominent lower lip which, if gently squeezed and released, opens and closes the flower's 'jaws', earning the plant its common name. Autumn-sown plants flower early and continue until the autumn frosts, longer if they are brought inside before temperatures fall.

Plant type: Hardy or slightly tender perennial, often grown as an annual.

Season: Flowers early summer to mid-autumn.

Height: 15–90cm (6in–3ft).

Spread: 15–45cm (6–18in).

Positioning: Full sun. Shorter kinds 10cm (4in) apart in troughs or pots; tall ones massed 23cm (9in) apart or as dot plants in larger containers.

Care: Pot in mid- to late spring in soil-based compost. Water in thoroughly and keep moist. Apply general fertilizer every 10–14 days. Deadhead flower spikes. Discard plants in late autumn.

Propagation: Sow in a frame in autumn, or under glass in early spring; move seedlings to trays or pots.

Recommended: Tall: 'Liberty', 'Madam Butterfly'. Dwarf: 'Floral Carpet', 'Little Darling'. Intermediate: 'Cheerio', 'Cinderella'.

Useful tip: For earlier, longer flowering feed and deadhead autumn-sown plants kept in pots under glass.

Argyranthemum Marguerite, Paris Daisy

Plant type: Tender perennial shrub.

Season: Flowers early summer to mid-autumn.

Height: 60cm–1.2m (2–4ft).

Spread: 60–90cm (2–3ft).

Positioning: Full sun. As specimen bushes and standards in pots; massed 30–45cm (12–18in) apart as bedding in larger containers.

Care: Plant in multi-purpose compost with good drainage after the last frosts. Water in dry weather; liquid feed every 3–4 weeks. Support taller forms. Bring under cover in autumn; keep frost-free and barely moist. Prune to shape in spring, and pot on or top-dress.

Propagation: Grow cuttings under glass in mid-spring or late summer.

Recommended: 'Album Plenum' (double white), 'Qinta White', 'Jamaica Primrose', 'Rollason's Red', 'Petite Pink', 'Vancouver'.

Useful tip: Sow the perennial variety 'Whity' in early spring for growing as a tender annual.

ARGYRANTHEMUM SP.

As more varieties become available, the familiar marguerite (*A. frutescens*), once just a white daisy with a golden eye, has become a colourful collector's plant. All the many forms look superb in pots, particularly larger plants and standards when they are 3–4 years old and have bushy heads of flowering stems. (syn. *Chrysanthemum frutescens*.)

11

Aubrieta deltoidea Aubr(i)etia, Purple Rock-cress

AUBRIETA DELTOIDEA 'OAKINGTON LAVENDER'

Grow this around the edges of larger containers to soften their lines with dense cascades of neat grey-green or variegated foliage. Early in the season the whole plant disappears beneath masses of small red, purple or lilac flowers that stand out well against the predominantly yellow shades of spring. Most of the many varieties are very vigorous and need a firm trim annually.

Plant type:	Hardy evergreen trailing perennial.
Season:	Flowers early spring to early summer; foliage all year.
Height:	10–13cm (4–5in).
Spread:	Up to 60cm (2ft).
Positioning:	Full sun. As edging and ground cover in well-drained troughs, tubs and pots.
Care:	Plant in autumn or spring in soil-based compost with extra drainage. Water plants until established. Feed in late spring with slow-release pellets. After flowering trim off deadheads and cut back to a neat shape.
Propagation:	Divide named varieties in autumn or grow cuttings in a frame in summer; sow mixtures under glass in spring.
Recommended:	'Aureovariegata' (gold-edged), 'Bob Saunders' (double), violet 'Doctor Mules', 'Greencourt Purple', 'Novalis Blue', 'Red Carpet', white 'Argenteovariegata'.
Useful tip:	Use limestone chippings for drainage or as a surface mulch.

Begonia Begonia

Plant type: Tender herbaceous perennial; fibrous-rooted or tuberous.

Season: Flowers early summer to mid-autumn.

Height: 15–45cm (6–18in).

Spread: 15–45cm (6–18in).

Positioning: Light or semi-shade. 15–30cm (6–12in) apart in tubs and pots; trailing kinds in hanging baskets and window-boxes.

Care: Start tubers in early spring in trays of compost under glass; move to pots when growth appears. Plant all kinds after last frosts in multi-purpose compost. Water in dry weather; liquid feed occasionally. Dry tubers after flowering, store in a frost-free place over winter.

Propagation: Surface-sow under glass in mid-winter.

Recommended: *B. semperflorens* (Bedding Begonia); *B. × tuberhybrida*, smaller Multiflora hybrids; Pendula types and *B. sutherlandii* in hanging baskets.

Useful tip: Support large-flowered kinds with twiggy sticks.

BEGONIA × TUBERHYBRIDA 'NON-STOP'

Begonias are some of the most reliable summer bedding plants, particularly for containers in shade where their brilliant flowers and shapely foliage create luxuriant highlights all season. The largest tuberous-rooted hybrids are in a class of their own – their extravagant double blooms may reach 15cm (6in) across.

Bellis perennis (Double) Daisy

BELLIS PERENNIS 'MEDICI'

The dainty small-flowered varieties once favoured for spring bedding were eclipsed for a while by giant double forms with blooms 5cm (2in) across. Fashion has changed again and the future for the old miniatures now seems bright, especially in their role as patio plants for edging and underplanting in tubs and window-boxes.

Plant type: Hardy perennial, usually grown as a biennial bedding plant.

Season: Flowers early spring to mid-summer.

Height: 8–15cm (3–6in).

Spread: 15cm (6in).

Positioning: Full sun or partial shade. 15cm (6in) apart as bedding for edging tubs, window-boxes and hanging baskets.

Care: Plant in autumn in multi-purpose compost; water in well in dry weather. Apply general fertilizer in early spring. Dead-head regularly. Divide after flowering and transplant divisions to another site to grow on until autumn.

Propagation: Sow outdoors in early summer; divide clumps after flowering.

Recommended: Large-flowered 'Goliath', 'Monstrosa'; miniature 'Carpet' series, 'Pomponette' mixtures, 'Dresden China', 'Rob Roy'; 'Prolifera'.

Useful tip: Home-saved seeds may yield some single white 'wild' plants.

Bidens aurea Tickseed

BIDENS AUREA

Plant type: Tender evergreen perennial, often grown as a half-hardy annual.

Season: Flowers early summer to mid-autumn.

Height: 90cm (3ft), often less.

Spread: 90cm (3ft).

Positioning: Full sun, sheltered from cold winds. As a semi-trailer in window-boxes and hanging baskets; bedding in troughs, tubs.

Care: Plant after the last frosts in soil-based compost with extra drainage. Water moderately in dry weather; liquid feed every 2 weeks during flowering. Pinch young plants once or twice. After flowering take cuttings; discard main plants or pot up and keep barely moist over winter at 5°C (41°F) for spring cuttings.

Propagation: Grow cuttings under glass in spring, summer, early autumn.

Recommended: *B. ferulifolia*, basic species and 'Golden Goddess'; *B. aurea*, basic species only.

Useful tip: Give cuttings a little more heat than old plants over winter.

Two species of this splendid free-flowering perennial from Mexico are usually available. Both are attractive additions to summer bedding schemes, especially when planted so that they can infiltrate fuchsias and marguerites with long slender branches, each of which bears a profusion of bright yellow or gold daisies.

Brachycome iberidifolia Swan River Daisy

BRACHYCOME IBERIDIFOLIA 'PURPLE SPLENDOUR'

This delightful Australian species must usually be raised from seed. The feathery seedlings soon branch into bushy plants that almost flower themselves to exhaustion, especially in a very hot summer. The wiry stems eventually trail gracefully, making them useful for edging in containers.

Plant type: Slightly tender perennial, usually grown as a half-hardy annual.

Season: Flowers early summer to mid-autumn.

Height: 23–30cm (9–12in).

Spread: 15–23cm (6–9in).

Positioning: Full sun or very light shade, sheltered from winds. 20cm (8in) apart as bedding or edging in pots, troughs and baskets.

Care: Plant in late spring in soil-based compost. Water well in dry weather. Allow to trail or support stems with twiggy sticks. Dead-head once or twice in late summer, when 1–2 liquid feeds can also prolong flowers. Move to cooler site in hot summers.

Propagation: Sow seeds under glass in early spring; transplant to trays.

Recommended: Basic species and 'Purple Splendour', 'Blue Gleam', 'White Splendour'; hybrids 'Harmony', 'Tinkerbell'.

Useful tip: Sow a second batch of seeds in situ in late spring as hot summers may curtail flowering.

Calluna vulgaris Common Heather, Ling

Plant type: Hardy perennial evergreen shrub.

Season: Flowers mid-summer to late autumn; foliage all year round.

Height: 20–45cm (8–18in).

Spread: 45–90cm (18in–3ft).

Positioning: Full sun, away from dripping overhead foliage. 30cm (12in) apart in pots, troughs, sinks, window-boxes.

Care: Plant in spring or autumn in ericaceous (lime-free) compost: set foliage at surface level. Water well initially, then in very dry weather. Feed with rhododendron fertilizer in spring, mulch with composted bark. Trim after flowering, or leave over winter and clip in spring. Repot every 4–5 years in spring.

Propagation: Grow cuttings in a frame in spring and early summer.

Recommended: 'Gold Mist', 'Golden Carpet', 'Silver Knight', 'Sunset', 'Wickwar Flame', 'Beoley Gold'.

Useful tip: Winter-flowering *Erica carnea* provides out-of-season colour.

CALLUNA VULGARIS 'GOLD MIST'

Summer and autumn are the seasons for heather, when the dense compact plants burst into flowers in various bright shades. The tidy foliage is often as colourful as the blooms, especially when temperatures begin to fall. There is a host of varieties, all easy to grow in containers where they can be given the acid conditions that they prefer.

CAMELLIA × WILLIAMSII 'NOVEMBER PARK'

When grown in containers, camellias can be given the lime-free soil they prefer and provided with shelter when appropriate – although they are very hardy, flower buds may be injured by frost combined with early morning sunshine. If pots cannot be moved in frosty weather, protect buds with layers of fleece to guarantee a profusion of blooms.

Plant type:	Hardy perennial evergreen shrub or small tree.
Season:	Flowers early winter to late spring.
Height:	Up to 1.8m (6ft).
Spread:	1.8m (6ft).
Positioning:	Light shade, sheltered from cold winds, rising sun. As a specimen shrub in a tub or box.
Care:	Plant in spring in ericaceous (lime-free) compost with good drainage. Water with rainwater in dry weather, especially as buds begin to form; avoid waterlogging. Feed with liquid tomato fertilizer every 2–3 weeks until late summer. Deadhead; prune to shape after flowering. Top-dress in spring with well-rotted manure.
Propagation:	Grow cuttings in a frame in late summer.
Recommended:	*C. japonica* 'Alba Simplex', 'Berenice Boddy', 'Elegans'; *C. × williamsii* 'Debbie', 'Donation', 'Saint Ewe'.
Useful tip:	Plants grow well in an enclosed yard or basement area.

Plant type: Hardy evergreen prostrate perennial.

Season: Flowers late spring to mid-summer; foliage all year.

Height: 15cm (6in).

Spread: 60cm (2ft) or more.

Positioning: Full sun. 23–30cm (9–12in) apart in large pots, hanging baskets, window-boxes, and as ground cover or annual bedding.

Care: Plant in early spring in soil-based compost with extra drainage. Water now and then in dry weather. Trim after flowering, also in autumn if invasive. Feed in spring with slow-release pellets. For annual bedding, plant divisions in pots in late summer; overwinter in a frame.

Propagation: Divide clumps in spring or late summer; sow seeds under glass in early spring.

Recommended: Basic species and 'Silberteppich'; also *C. arvense* 'Compactum'.

Useful tip: Grow in the sunniest spots to encourage the whitest foliage.

CERASTIUM TOMENTOSUM 'YO-YO'

Silvery-white Cerastium is notorious for spreading irresistibly and overwhelming everything in its path. This is true when plants are mistakenly added to a rock garden, but restrained in containers they are well-behaved as early summer trailers and ground cover. They may also be grown as annual bedding plants for clearing after flowering.

Cheiranthus cheiri Wallflower

CHEIRANTHUS CHEIRI MIXTURE

Plant type: Hardy perennial evergreen subshrub, usually grown as a biennial.

Season: Flowers early spring to early summer.

Height: 23–60cm (9in–2ft).

Spread: 15–30cm (6–12in).

Positioning: Full sun. As bedding, 20–30cm (8–12in) apart, in tubs, troughs.

Care: Plant in mid-autumn or late winter, firmly in soil-based compost with extra drainage; pinch out growing tips. In spring, tidy broken or dead branches; top-dress with general fertilizer or feed with slow-release pellets. Discard after flowering.

Propagation: Sow outdoors in limed soil in early summer; thin or transplant seedlings to 8cm (3in) apart.

Recommended: Large-flowered: 'Blood Red', 'Cloth of Gold'. Intermediate: 'Orange Bedder', 'Scarlet Bedder'. Dwarf: 'Tom Thumb Mixed'.

Useful tip: The Siberian Wallflower, *C. allionii* (syn. *Erysimum* × *allionii*), blooms about a month or so later.

This is the traditional spring bedding plant for massing in tubs near the house, where the fragrance of its brilliant flowers can be enjoyed in the early sunshine. Colours range from ivory white to deep purple, with yellow and red shades predominating. Firm planting is essential to prevent tall spindly stems from developing. (syn. *Erysimum cheiri*.)

Choisya ternata Mexican Orange Blossom

Plant type: Hardy or slightly tender evergreen perennial shrub.

Season: Foliage all year; flowers mid- to late spring, occasionally in autumn.

Height: 1.5–2.7m (5–9ft).

Spread: 1.5–1.8m (5–6ft).

Positioning: Dappled sunlight or light shade, sheltered from cold winds. As a specimen in a tub or large pot by a wall.

Care: Plant in spring or early summer in soil-based compost. Water in dry weather. Cut back some older branches after flowering. Move containers into shelter in autumn. Pot on small plants annually in spring; top-dress mature specimens.

Propagation: Grow cuttings under glass in early summer, in a frame in autumn.

Recommended: Basic species and greenish-gold 'Sundance'; also hybrid C. 'Aztec Pearl', with pink buds.

Useful tip: In autumn protect exposed plants that are too large to move with hessian sacking or layers of fleece.

CHOISYA TERNATA 'SUNDANCE'

Although nominally hardy, the aromatic foliage of this Mexican evergreen, especially gold forms, is easily scorched by cold winds or a combination of frost and sunshine. Be prepared to move containers into a sheltered position in winter, where plants will repay the extra care with more prolific flowering.

CLEMATIS MONTANA VAR. WILSONII

Plant type:	Hardy deciduous perennial climber.
Season:	Between mid-spring and mid-autumn.
Height:	1.8m (6ft) or more.
Spread:	90cm–1.2m (3–4ft).
Positioning:	Full sun, with roots in the shade; in 30cm (12in) pots or in threes on wooden tripods in larger pots and tubs.
Care:	Plant in mid-autumn or spring in soil-based compost with extra drainage; bury crowns 8–10cm (3–4in) below surface. Water regularly, daily when hot; liquid feed fortnightly during growth. Train stems to trellis, canes, wires. Prune according to variety, usually after flowering. Top-dress in spring; repot every 4–5 years.
Propagation:	Grow cuttings under glass in summer.
Recommended:	Most large-flowered kinds; small-flowered Alpina, Macropetala, Viticella hybrids; *C. armandii*, forms of *C. montana* benefit from a warm wall.
Useful tip:	Grow with a rose like 'Danse du Feu'.

Clematis are always supplied as pot-grown plants, so it is a simple matter to move one on into a medium-size pot for permanent container cultivation. In larger tubs and troughs, it may be grown with a long-flowering climbing rose for a dramatic partnership. Plants flower between mid-spring and mid-autumn, depending on variety.

Corylus avellana 'Contorta' Corkscrew Hazel

Plant type: Hardy deciduous perennial shrub or small tree.

Season: Catkins in late winter; stems all year.

Height: 2.4–3m (8–10ft).

Spread: Up to 1.8m (6ft).

Positioning: Full sun or semi-shade, sheltered from strong winds at flowering time. As a specimen tree in a tub or half-barrel.

Care: Plant in autumn or spring in soil-based compost, in a large pot for the first year, then in the final container. Water now and then in dry weather; liquid feed monthly from flowering time to late summer. Top-dress in early winter. Cut back one-year old stems after flowering for the first 5 years, thereafter completely remove one stem in 3 every 2–3 years. Watch out for aphids in summer.

Propagation: Layer, or sow seeds in a frame, in autumn.

Recommended: This variety only.

Useful tip: In winter stand where the stems and catkins will be outlined against the sky.

CORYLUS AVELLANA 'CONTORTA'

Winter is the corkscrew hazel's season of glory, when the curiously twisted stems that earn it the alternative name 'Harry Lauder's walking-stick' stand out in a delicate tracery. In late winter golden catkins deck the bare branches.

COTONEASTER MICROPHYLLUS

Shiny leaves and white flowers are tiny and perfectly shaped, and are carried on stiffly spreading stems. Mature plants form open mounds that arch gracefully on all sides of a container, making an attractive feature in the open, but the branches may also be trained flat against a wall as an evergreen background.

Plant type: Hardy perennial evergreen shrub; semi-prostrate.

Season: Flowers late spring; berries in autumn; foliage all year.

Height: 60–90cm (2–3ft)

Spread: Up to 1.8m (6ft).

Positioning: Full sun. In large pots or troughs where stems can arch or be trained on a wall.

Care: Plant in autumn or winter in soil-based compost. Top-dress in spring or feed with slow-release pellets. Remove dead wood and unwanted branches in winter; trim to shape in mid-spring.

Propagation: Grow cuttings under glass in summer or in a frame in autumn and winter.

Recommended: Basic species only – 'Donard Gem' and 'Teulon Porter' are now *C. astrophorus*; *C. horizontalis*; *C. conspicuus* 'Decorus'; *C. salicifolius* 'Pendulus'.

Useful tip: Quality varies, so buy specimens with the best berries in autumn.

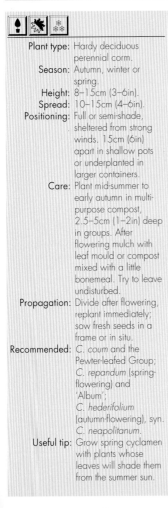

Plant type: Hardy deciduous perennial corm.

Season: Autumn, winter or spring.

Height: 8–15cm (3–6in).

Spread: 10–15cm (4–6in).

Positioning: Full or semi-shade, sheltered from strong winds. 15cm (6in) apart in shallow pots or underplanted in larger containers.

Care: Plant mid-summer to early autumn in multi-purpose compost, 2.5–5cm (1–2in) deep in groups. After flowering mulch with leaf mould or compost mixed with a little bonemeal. Try to leave undisturbed.

Propagation: Divide after flowering, replant immediately; sow fresh seeds in a frame or in situ.

Recommended: *C. coum* and the Pewter-leafed Group; *C. repandum* (spring-flowering) and 'Album'; *C. hederifolium* (autumn-flowering), syn. *C. neapolitanum*.

Useful tip: Grow spring cyclamen with plants whose leaves will shade them from the summer sun.

CYCLAMEN HEDERIFOLIUM

Several charming species of wild small-flowered cyclamen are ideal for growing in containers, both on their own and beneath shrubs and small trees. An annual mulch of organic material imitates the leafy dressings cyclamen receive in their natural woodland surroundings. Take care not to disturb the shallow corms when you replace compost around shrubs.

Dahlia hybrids Dahlia

DAHLIA 'TINY TOT'

The bushy dahlia hybrids used for summer bedding in borders are easily grown in containers and give an exuberant display of brilliant colour, right up to the autumn frosts. All they ask is sunshine, plenty of water in dry weather, and the kind of rich diet provided by adding a little well-rotted manure to the container.

Plant type: Tender tuberous perennial, often grown as an annual.

Season: Mid-summer to first autumn frosts.

Height: 30–60cm (12–24in).

Spread: 30–45cm (12–18in).

Positioning: Full sun. 30cm (12in) apart as bedding in pots, troughs, tubs.

Care: Plant tubers 8cm (3in) deep in soil-based compost outdoors in mid-spring; or start in pots under glass in early spring, pot on and stand outside after the last frosts. Before planting spread well-rotted manure on the base of the pot or mix it with compost. Water regularly; liquid feed monthly. Deadhead. After first frosts cut off blackened stems, dig up and dry tubers. Store in a frost-proof place.

Propagation: Sow under glass in late winter; divide tubers before planting.

Recommended: 'Coltness Hybrids', 'Dandy', 'Redskin', 'Sunny Yellow'.

Useful tip: Stand drying tubers upside-down to drain water from the stems.

Plant type: Hardy perennial deciduous and evergreen shrubs.

Season: Mid-winter to mid-spring.

Height: 1.2m (4ft).

Spread: 90cm–1.2m (3–4ft).

Positioning: Dappled sunlight or semi-shade, sheltered from cold winds. As specimens in large deep pots or tubs.

Care: Plant in autumn or spring in multi-purpose or lime-free compost. Mulch with composted bark, and keep topped up. Feed in spring with slow-release pellets. Water regularly in dry weather. Cut out weak growth in spring or summer. Repot or plant out in the garden if growth declines.

Propagation: Grow cuttings in a frame in summer or layer in spring.

Recommended: Evergreen: *D. odora*, 'Aureomarginata'. Deciduous: *D. mezereum*, *alba* and var. *rubra*; *D. × burkwoodii*, 'Somerset'.

Useful tip: If too much lime turns leaves yellow, water with sequestered iron.

DAPHNE CNEORUM 'EXIMIA'

All daphnes are exceptionally beautiful in flower, and so fragrant that their perfume can be detected far across the garden. Most will grow in containers, but they are sometimes difficult to keep for many years: they detest drought – in the wild most root deeply in cool leafy soils – so regular watering is vital.

Euonymus fortunei Evergreen Euonymus

EUONYMUS FORTUNEI 'SILVER QUEEN'

Plant type:	Hardy perennial evergreen shrub.
Season:	Foliage all year.
Height:	90cm–1.5m (3–5ft).
Spread:	1.2–1.5m (4–5ft).
Positioning:	Full sun or semi-shade. In tubs, half-barrels as specimens, topiary, wall shrubs.
Care:	Plant in autumn or spring in soil-based compost with extra drainage and cut back by one-third. Water in dry weather; feed once or twice with high-potash fertilizer. Trim to shape in spring, topiary again in mid-summer. Remove one stem in 3 from old plants every spring. Top-dress in spring.
Propagation:	Grow cuttings under glass in summer, in a frame in winter.
Recommended:	'Blondy', 'Emerald Gaiety', 'Emerald 'n' Gold', 'Silver Queen', 'Sun Spot'; also more vigorous *E. japonicus*, and 'Aureus', 'Duc d'Anjou', 'Latifolius Albomarginatus'.
Useful tip:	Mildew is encouraged if pots dry out; prune affected shoots and keep plants moist.

Several varieties of this robust shrub are suitable for a multitude of forms in pots on a patio: plants can be trained on walls, clipped to formal geometrical shapes or simply allowed to spread naturally. In full sun their colours glow intensely, but they also make luminous highlights in relatively dull corners.

Fargesia nitida Fountain Bamboo

Plant type: Hardy perennial evergreen shrub.

Season: Foliage all year.

Height: 3–4m (10–13ft).

Spread: 3m (10ft); limited by container.

Positioning: Partial or full shade, sheltered from extreme frost. As a specimen clump in a large deep tub or half-barrel.

Care: In autumn or spring plant single plants in large pots or 3 in a tub. Water well in dry weather; liquid feed every 6–8 weeks from early spring to mid-autumn. Top-dress in spring. If space is limited trim tops and sides of mature clumps. After 3–4 years, remove some of the oldest canes in spring.

Propagation: Divide clumps in late spring.

Recommended: Basic species and 'Nymphenburg', 'Eisenach'. Also *F. murieliae*, syn. *Sinarundinaria murieliae* (Umbrella Bamboo), similar with light pea-green stems.

Useful tip: Use dried 3-year-old stems as canes.

FARGESIA NITIDA

This elegant bamboo expands slowly into a dense clump of arching purple-flushed stems, with delicate 10cm (4in) leaves that ripple gracefully in the breeze. (syns *Arundinaria*, *Phyllostachys* and *Sinarundinaria nitida*.)

Fatsia japonica Japanese Aralia

FATSIA JAPONICA

A showy evergreen that usually grows wider than it is tall, Fatsia is ideal for filling a shaded corner with its spreading branches and evenly spaced palm-shaped leaves, which can reach 38cm (15in) across or more, on long elegant stalks. Their polished surface gleams in subdued light. Established plants are very hardy.

Plant type: Hardy or slightly tender perennial evergreen shrub.

Season: Flowers in autumn; fruits in spring; foliage all year.

Height: 1.5–1.8m (5–6ft).

Spread: 1.8m (6ft).

Positioning: Dappled sunlight to semi-shade, sheltered from cold winds. As a specimen in a large tub or half-barrel.

Care: Plant in spring in multi-purpose compost with extra drainage. Water regularly in dry weather; liquid feed every 4–6 weeks from spring to autumn. Top-dress mature plants in spring. In late spring, cut out some of the oldest branches, shorten others, if necessary.

Propagation: Grow cuttings under glass in spring and summer.

Recommended: Basic species and 'Moseri', and variegated 'Aurea', 'Albomarginata'.

Useful tip: To protect young plants from frost, wrap pots in bubble plastic and cover top growth with fleece.

Felicia amelloides
Kingfisher Daisy, Blue Marguerite

Plant type: Tender perennial evergreen shrub, often grown as a half-hardy annual.

Season: Flowers mid-summer to early autumn.

Height: 30–45cm (12–18in).

Spread: 23–30cm (9–12in).

Positioning: Full sun, sheltered from strong winds. As specimen pot plants; 23cm (9in) apart in tubs as bedding.

Care: Grow in pots of soil-based compost. After the last frosts, plunge pots to the rim in larger containers or stand them outdoors; pinch out tips. Water regularly; deadhead; liquid feed every 3–4 weeks when flowering. Take cuttings in autumn and grow on indoors, or overwinter, barely moist, under frost-free glass.

Propagation: Grow cuttings under glass in spring, summer or autumn.

Recommended: Basic species and 'Read's White', 'Santa Anita Variegated'.

Useful tip: *F. bergeriana*, a dwarf annual form, is raised from seeds sown in heat in early spring.

FELICIA AMELLOIDES 'READ'S BLUE'

This exceptionally beautiful blue-flowered daisy from South Africa may be grown as a cool conservatory plant for standing outside between the first and last frosts. Since cuttings root very easily, plants can also be treated as annual bedding for sunny parts of the patio, where they make a fine display all summer. (syns *Agathaea coelestis*, *F. capensis*.)

Fritillaria imperialis Crown Imperial

FRITILLARIA IMPERIALIS 'RUBRA MAXIMA'

Most Fritillaries thrive in containers, where species sensitive to winter damp can be brought under cover. Crown imperials are happy in all weathers outdoors, and develop into small clumps of stately stems bearing large bells in eye-catching shades of yellow, orange or red. Try underplanting with snakeshead fritillaries, their dwarf relatives.

Plant type: Hardy perennial deciduous bulb.

Season: Flowers mid- and late spring.

Height: 60–90cm (2–3ft).

Spread: 23–30cm (9–12in).

Positioning: Sun or semi-shade. 10–15cm (4–6in) apart in groups in large pots and tubs.

Care: Plant in autumn, 15–20cm (6–8in) deep in soil-based compost with extra drainage; lay bulbs on their sides to prevent rotting. Water in dry weather; liquid feed once or twice after flowering and before the foliage dies down. Deadhead if seeds are not required. Top-dress in spring.

Propagation: Sow ripe seeds in a frame; detach offsets after flowering and pot up immediately.

Recommended: Basic species and bright orange 'Aurora', yellow 'Maxima Lutea', 'Rubra', variegated 'Aureomarginata'; also *F. persica* 'Adiyaman', and *F. meleagris* (Snakeshead Fritillary).

Useful tip: Do not disturb bulbs for at least 3–4 years.

Fuchsia Fuchsia

FUCHSIA 'LOVE'S REWARD'

Plant type:	Hardy or slightly tender perennial deciduous shrub.
Season:	Flowers early summer to early autumn.
Height:	Up to 1.5m (5ft).
Spread:	60–90cm (2–3ft).
Positioning:	Full sun or light shade, sheltered from winds. Standards, bushes in pots, tubs; trailers in hanging baskets.
Care:	Plant in multi-purpose compost, hardy kinds in spring, tender ones after the last frosts. Water freely in dry weather. Top-dress hardy kinds in spring; liquid feed all plants every 7–10 days when flowering. Bring tender varieties indoors in autumn, keep barely moist and repot in spring; cut down hardy plants in late autumn.
Propagation:	Grow cuttings under glass in spring and summer.
Recommended:	Hardy: *F. magellanica* and 'Alba', 'Gracilis'; also dwarf 'Tom Thumb'. Tender: 'Cascade' (baskets); 'Annabel' (bush).
Useful tip:	Mulch hardy kinds against frost.

Fuchsias are justly popular for their often dramatic displays of bright flowers and both hardy and tender kinds may be grown in containers. They are an excellent choice for light shade, and many varieties can be trained as standards to provide imaginative summer centrepieces.

Gaultheria procumbens (Creeping) Wintergreen, Chequerberry

GAULTHERIA PROCUMBENS 'MACROCARPA'

The dense evergreen carpets of neat foliage that distinguish this spreading North American shrublet begin to turn colour as autumn advances. They assume rich bronze and reddish tints, which complement bright red berries that are as aromatic as the foliage. Altogether a choice, and usually undemanding, ground-cover plant to grow with acid-loving specimens in larger permanent containers.

Plant type: Hardy perennial evergreen shrub; creeping stems.

Season: Flowers in summer; berries in autumn; foliage all year.

Height: 50cm (20in).

Spread: Up to 2.4m (8ft); limited by container.

Positioning: Light or semi-shade. In pots, tubs, half-barrels as ground cover with acid-loving shrubs, small trees.

Care: Plant in autumn or spring in soil-less lime-free compost. Water in dry weather (ideally with rainwater); liquid feed once or twice in summer. In spring prune dead or straggly stems and top-dress with fresh compost or leaf mould.

Propagation: Grow cuttings in a frame in summer; remove rooted layers in spring.

Recommended: Basic species only; G. × wisleyensis (formerly × Gaulnettya) hybrids 'Pink Pixie', 'Wisley Pearl'.

Useful tip: Red-tinted leaves at any time other than winter indicate stress, usually lack of water.

Hebe Shrubby Veronica

Plant type: Hardy or slightly tender perennial evergreen shrub.

Season: Flowers early summer to autumn, according to variety; foliage all year.

Height: 60cm–1.2m (2–4ft).

Spread: 60–90cm (2–3ft).

Positioning: Full sun, sheltered from strong winds, hard frost. Dwarf kinds in troughs and window-boxes; others in tubs.

Care: Plant in autumn or late spring in multi-purpose compost with extra drainage. Water freely in dry weather; avoid waterlogging. Trim after flowering; prune leggy shrubs hard in spring. In autumn move less hardy kinds to a sheltered spot or under glass. In spring top-dress, feed with slow-release pellets.

Propagation: Grow cuttings under glass in late spring or in a frame in autumn.

Recommended: *H. buchananii* and 'Minor'; *H. pinguifolia* and 'Pagei'; also *H.* 'Carl Teschner'.

Useful tip: Watch out for aphids in summer and mildew in autumn.

HEBE 'AUTUMN GLORY'

Many of the various Hebes make excellent container plants because their evergreen foliage is always neat and satisfying, while their lilac, purple or white flowers are pretty and prolific. Smaller varieties are often the hardiest and easiest to grow: always choose a sunny warm position, ideally against a sheltered wall.

Hedera helix Common Ivy, English Ivy

Plant type:	Hardy perennial evergreen climber/trailer.
Season:	Flowers then berries in early autumn; foliage all year.
Height:	90cm–9m (3–30ft).
Spread:	60cm–5m (2–16ft).
Positioning:	Full sun or shade. Permanent plants in tubs against a wall or fence; seasonal ones in window-boxes, tubs or hanging baskets.
Care:	Plant in autumn or spring, singly or 30cm (12in) apart, in soil-based compost. Water in dry weather; liquid feed monthly in spring, summer. Let stems trail, or tie to canes until self-supporting. Trim in late summer or spring. Repot small plants every other year; top-dress large containers in spring.
Propagation:	Grow cuttings in a frame in summer.
Recommended:	'Buttercup', 'Cristata'. Walls: H. hibernica 'Deltoidea', 'Gracilis'; H. algeriensis 'Gloire de Marengo'.
Useful tip:	Variegated kinds need some sun; green ones tolerate full shade.

HEDERA HELIX 'GOLDHEART'

There is hardly a site in which these versatile plants will not thrive. As climbers they can be grown in the usual way and will almost reach their normal full height – anything from 90cm (3ft) to 9m (30ft) depending on variety – in containers, but many also have great potential as trailers. Grow choice named forms as permanent edging to drape the sides of tubs, or as winter and spring bedding.

Helichrysum italicum Curry Plant

Plant type: Hardy or slightly tender perennial evergreen shrub.

Season: Flowers in summer; foliage all year.

Height: 60cm (2ft).

Spread: 30–60cm (1–2ft).

Positioning: Full sun, protected from frost and cold winds. As a specimen shrub in tubs or pots.

Care: Plant in spring in soil-based compost with extra drainage. Water occasionally in very dry weather; feed with rose fertilizer in spring and summer. Trim flowering stems as they appear if desired; prune lightly to shape in spring. Top-dress in spring. Screen plants and insulate pots In a hard winter, or move to a cool greenhouse or conservatory.

Propagation: Grow cuttings under glass in summer.

Recommended: Basic species and ssp. *microphyllum* and 'Nanum', both dwarf; also *H. stoechas* and dwarf 'White Barn'.

Useful tip: Plants may be trimmed to a neat outline, but never cut back into old wood.

HELICHRYSUM ITALICUM

This is a plant that invites handling to release the spicy fragrance of its bright silvery-white foliage, especially when it has been warmed by the sun, so position it where it is brushed in passing. It is a culinary and cosmetic herb, also popular with flower arrangers: the tight rounded flower buds can be dried, and open blooms last well in water. (syn. *H. angustifolium*.)

39

Helichrysum petiolare
Liquorice Plant, Helichrysum

HELICHRYSUM PETIOLARE

This slightly stiff shrub, a popular trailing plant for hanging baskets and summer bedding containers, is best known in its basic silver-grey form. However, prettily coloured variants are also available and are even more attractive, both as edging plants and planted on the surface to infiltrate other patio shrubs. Flowers are insignificant. (syn. *H. petiolaris*.)

Plant type: Slightly tender perennial evergreen shrub.

Season: Flowers in summer; foliage all year.

Height: 30cm (12in).

Spread: 90cm–1.2m (3–4ft).

Positioning: Full sun or semi-shade. Singly or 30–45cm (12–18in) apart as trailers in hanging baskets and window-boxes and as edging in larger tubs.

Care: Plant after the last frosts in multi-purpose compost. Water regularly in dry weather; liquid feed every 3–4 weeks. Trim branches if needed in summer. Bring under cover before frosts and cut back hard, or take cuttings and discard plants. Repot in spring.

Propagation: Grow cuttings under glass from late spring to early autumn.

Recommended: Basic species; also 'Goring Silver', 'Roundabout', 'Variegatum'.

Useful tip: *H. microphyllum* (syn. *Plectostachys serpyllifolia*) is ideal in smaller containers: trim straggling stems.

Hyacinthus orientalis Common Hyacinth

Plant type:	Hardy perennial deciduous bulb.
Season:	Flowers early and mid-spring.
Height:	15–30cm (6–12in).
Spread:	15–20cm (6–8in).
Positioning:	Full sun or very light shade. As permanent underplanting or bedding around shrubs in pots, tubs, window-boxes.
Care:	Plant untreated ('bedding') bulbs in early autumn, 15cm (6in) deep and 10–15cm (4–6in) apart, in multi-purpose compost. Support tall flower stems with thin canes. Let foliage die down naturally, then lift bulbs for drying and storing until autumn; or leave undisturbed.
Propagation:	Detach small offsets from bulbs in autumn; replant immediately.
Recommended:	Dutch hybrids include 'Anna Marie' (pink), 'Blue Jacket', 'City of Haarlem' (yellow), 'L'Innocence' (white); also Multiflora hybrids.
Useful tip:	Large prepared or heat-treated bulbs only flower indoors in their first season.

HYACINTHUS ORIENTALIS 'HOLLYHOCK'

Many different varieties of hyacinth are popular for forcing into flower indoors, but the same kinds can also be planted outside. There the blooms are neater and more compact, and often last longer, filling a sunny corner of the patio with their fragrance for weeks on end. Force prepared bulbs in bowls indoors and move them outside in future seasons to get the best of both methods.

Hydrangea macrophylla Hydrangea

HYDRANGEA MACROPHYLLA VAR.

These are excellent late-flowering shrubs for large containers, especially glazed or plastic types (line porous pots with polythene to reduce water loss). Plenty of water and nourishment encourage vigorous growth and lavish blooms over a long season; the dead flower heads remain decorative well after any colour has faded.

Plant type: Hardy perennial deciduous shrub.

Season: Flowers mid-summer to early autumn.

Height: 1.2–1.8m (4–6ft).

Spread: 1.2–1.8m (4–6ft).

Positioning: Light shade, sheltered from frost and early morning sunlight. As specimen bushes in large pots and tubs.

Care: Plant in autumn or spring in multi-purpose compost (lime-free for blue flowers). Mulch with a composted bark mixture or well-rotted manure; liquid feed every 2–3 weeks. In dry weather water freely. Deadhead in spring, prune lightly to shape: cut out dead, weak, crowded stems. Top-dress in spring.

Propagation: Grow cuttings under glass in summer.

Recommended: Hortensia (Mophead): 'Ami Pasquier', 'Mme Emile Mouillère', 'Ayesha', 'Générale Vicomtesse de Vibraye', 'Parzifal'. Lacecap: 'Geoffrey Chadbund'.

Useful tip: Grow climbing H. petiolaris in a tub against a shaded wall.

Ilex aquifolium Common Holly, English Holly

Plant type: Hardy perennial evergreen shrub or small tree.

Season: Berries in autumn and winter; foliage all year.

Height: 4m (13ft).

Spread: 1.8m (6ft).

Positioning: Full sun or shade, sheltered from cold winds. As specimens and trained standards in pots and tubs.

Care: Plant in autumn or spring in soil-based compost. Water well after planting and during dry weather. Liquid feed every 4–6 weeks. Trim to shape in late spring, formal shrubs and topiary again in late summer. Top-dress in spring.

Propagation: Grow cuttings in a frame in autumn.

Recommended: Female: 'Argentea Marginata', 'Madame Briot', 'Handsworth New Silver'; also *I. × altaclarensis* 'Lawsoniana'. Male: 'Ferox Argentea', 'Golden Queen'. Self-fertile: 'J. C. van Tol'.

Useful tip: For plenty of berries, choose a self-fertile kind or grow a male variety near females.

ILEX AQUIFOLIUM 'GOLDEN QUEEN'

Hollies are hardy, evergreen and responsive to clipping, qualities that recommend these tough shrubs for container cultivation. Variegated fruiting kinds (female or self-fertile) are the most attractive and can be used to brighten gloomy corners.

Impatiens walleriana Busy Lizzie

IMPATIENS WALLERIANA MIXTURE

Few other bedding plants provide such a continuous and weather-resistant parade of colour all season. Busy Lizzies are equally happy in sun or shade, although the largest plants and best displays occur in cool moist semi-shade where most other plants will sulk. Plant them liberally, and remember that they will continue flowering under glass if kept warm enough.

Plant type: Tender perennial evergreen succulent, often grown as an annual.

Season: Flowers early summer to early autumn.

Height: 15–45cm (6–18in).

Spread: 15–45cm (6–18in).

Positioning: Full sun or semi-shade. As specimens in pots; 15–23cm (6–9in) apart in larger containers as bedding.

Care: Plant after the last frosts in multi-purpose compost. Water in dry weather; liquid feed fortnightly. Pinch out tips occasionally. After flowering discard, or bring indoors before frosts and keep warm – do not overwater. In spring trim to shape and repot.

Propagation: Grow cuttings under glass from late spring to late summer.

Recommended: Tall: Accent, Tempo. Dwarf: Blitz, Deco. Also 'Starbright' (bi-coloured); 'Rosette' (double flowers); New Guinea hybrids (more tender).

Useful tip: Grow trailing 'Futura' in window-boxes and hanging baskets.

Plant type: Hardy perennial deciduous bulb.

Season: Flowers mid- or late winter to early spring.

Height: 15cm (6in).

Spread: 8–10cm (3–4in).

Positioning: Full sun (earliest flowers) or very light shade. In permanent groups in troughs, pots, window-boxes.

Care: Plant in early or mid-autumn, 8cm (3in) deep and 5–8cm (2–3in) apart, in soil-based compost with extra drainage; protect pots from freezing. After flowering, liquid feed every 3–4 weeks until foliage dies down. In late winter top-dress with bonemeal.

Propagation: Divide clumps after flowering, separate tiny bulblets and replant in separate containers.

Recommended: Basic species and seedling mixtures; also 'Alba', 'Cantab', 'Harmony', 'Joyce', 'Royal Blue', 'Violet Beauty'; *I. histrioides* 'Major'.

Useful tip: Do not disturb bulbs for at least 4–5 years.

IRIS RETICULATA 'CANTAB'

Dainty colourful flowers can start appearing as early as mid-winter when these irises are grown in a sunny warm position. Plants are reliable and inexpensive, making them a good choice for massing lavishly in containers of all kinds; because of their diminutive size they are particularly suitable for window-boxes and alpine troughs.

JUNIPERUS HORIZONTALIS 'MONTANA'

Dwarf and slow-growing junipers are important conifers for growing in containers. They come in a huge range of lovely forms and colours, and are undemanding plants that can withstand frost, wind and even a certain amount of neglect without injury. Most will thrive for many years in a medium-size pot.

Plant type: Hardy perennial evergreen conifer.

Season: Foliage all year.

Height: Up to 3m (10ft), according to variety.

Spread: Up to 1.5m (5ft).

Positioning: Full sun or very light shade. As specimen foliage plants: dwarf kinds in alpine sinks, window-boxes, pots; slow-growing ones in tubs, half-barrels.

Care: Plant in autumn or spring in soil-based compost with extra drainage. Water in dry weather; liquid feed once or twice in summer. Trim to shape in late summer. Top-dress in spring with bark compost.

Propagation: Grow cuttings in a frame in autumn.

Recommended: Dwarf: *J. chinensis* 'Variegated Kaizuka', *J. horizontalis* 'Grey Pearl', *J. × media* 'Old Gold', *J. squamata* 'Blue Star'. Large: *J. communis* 'Gold Cone', *J. virginiana* 'Sky Rocket', *J.* 'Grey Owl'.

Useful tip: Golden varieties colour best in light shade, blue forms in full sun.

Lantana camara Yellow Sage, Shrub Verbena

Plant type: Tender perennial evergreen shrub.

Season: Flowers late spring to mid-autumn.

Height: 60–75cm (2–2½ ft), sometimes more.

Spread: 60cm (2ft).

Positioning: Full sun or very light shade. As specimens in hanging baskets, pots; massed 45cm (18in) apart in tubs; as standard dot plants.

Care: Plant after the last frosts in soil-less compost. Water freely in dry weather; liquid feed every 2–3 weeks in summer, autumn. Let stems trail or support with twiggy sticks. Prune to shape after flowering. In early autumn bring indoors and overwinter at 13°C (55°F), or discard after flowering.

Propagation: Grow cuttings under glass in spring and summer; sow under glass in early spring.

Recommended: Basic species, 'Hybrid Mixture' for sowing; also 'Firebrand', 'Gold Dust', 'Snow White'.

Useful tip: Pots may be buried to their rims in larger containers.

LANTANA CAMARA

Better known as short-lived house plants, these leafy shrubs enjoy a sunny position outdoors and look slightly tropical when grown in decorative pots on the patio. Their fragrant blooms, popular with butterflies, are like multi-coloured verbenas as they change gradually from yellow to orange or red.

Lilium Lily

LILIUM TIGRINUM 'SPLENDENS'

Lilies are traditional pot plants and will flower earlier or later in their first year, depending on when they were planted. They can stay in pots for several seasons if fed after flowering, and look spectacular when arranged in formal groups to flank a path or doorway. For a long season of bloom, choose varieties which flower in succession.

Plant type:	Hardy perennial deciduous bulb.
Season:	Early summer to early autumn.
Height:	Up to 1.5m (5ft).
Spread:	15–23cm (6–9in).
Positioning:	Full sun or light shade, sheltered from winds. Several bulbs in large pots, tubs; single ones in deep pots.
Care:	Plant in autumn or spring, 15cm (6in) deep and 10–15cm (4–6in) apart, in soil-based compost with extra drainage. Grow in light shade until growing well. Water in dry weather; liquid feed fortnightly from bud formation until a month after blooms fade. Support tall stems. Leave to die down naturally. Repot small plants in spring, top-dress others.
Propagation:	Divide in autumn.
Recommended:	L. martagon and 'Album'; L. candidum (Madonna Lily); L. pyrenaicum; L. speciosum; Asiatic and Aurelian hybrids.
Useful tip:	Plant Madonna and Martagon lilies only 5–8cm (2–3in) deep.

Lobelia erinus Lobelia

Plant type: Tender evergreen perennial, usually grown as a half-hardy annual.

Season: Early summer to mid-autumn.

Height: 10–15cm (4–6in).

Spread: 10–30cm (4–12in); or trailing to 45cm (18in).

Positioning: Full sun or very light shade. As bedding, 15cm (6in) apart, in pots, tubs, window-boxes and hanging baskets.

Care: Plant in multi-purpose compost in late spring. Keep consistently moist; liquid feed fortnightly. Plants are usually discarded, but may be overwintered in gentle heat for spring propagation.

Propagation: Surface-sow seeds under glass in early spring; prick out in small clusters.

Recommended: Bush: 'Crystal Palace', 'Cambridge Blue'. Trailing: var. *pendula*, 'Fountain' and 'Cascade' mixtures, 'Sapphire' (blue with white eye).

Useful tip: If flowering ceases, trim off growing tips to encourage more buds.

LOBELIA ERINUS MIXTURE

Summer bedding schemes depend on lobelia varieties for their bright conspicuous display of colour and also as a source of blue, a shade that is scarce among long-flowering annuals. Plants need plenty of moisture in a dry season and respond to regular attention with exuberant masses of blooms which, in trailing varieties, cascade delicately around the sides of containers.

Lobularia maritima Sweet Alyssum, Little Dorrit

LOBULARIA MARITIMA 'ROSIE O' DAY'

This old favourite for summer bedding schemes was once available only in white but now comes in several effective colours, separately or in attractive blends. In a still position the flowers produce a rich scent of honey which lingers in the warm air. If plants are kept moist, tiny flowers hide the neat cushions of foliage all summer.

Plant type: Hardy annual, sometimes hardy evergreen perennial.

Season: Flowers early summer to mid-autumn.

Height: 8–15cm (3–6in).

Spread: 15–45cm (6–18in).

Positioning: Full sun, tolerates light shade. As edging, 10–15cm (4-6in) apart, for troughs, tubs, window-boxes.

Care: Sow or plant in late spring in multi-purpose compost. Water often in a dry season; move to light shade in a prolonged hot spell. If flowering ceases, trim off old blooms with scissors and liquid feed once only to stimulate further flushes. Discard after flowering.

Propagation: Sow seeds in trays in a frame in late winter or in situ in mid- to late spring.

Recommended: 'Carpet of Snow', 'Snow Crystals'; coloured forms like 'Rosie O'Day', 'Royal Carpet'; also mixtures like 'Pastel Carpet', 'Wonderland'.

Useful tip: Avoid over-feeding as it encourages foliage instead of flowers.

Lotus berthelottii Coral Gem, Parrot's Beak

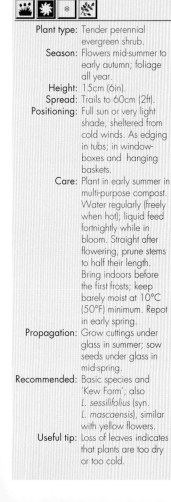

Plant type: Tender perennial evergreen shrub.

Season: Flowers mid-summer to early autumn; foliage all year.

Height: 15cm (6in).

Spread: Trails to 60cm (2ft).

Positioning: Full sun or very light shade, sheltered from cold winds. As edging in tubs; in window-boxes and hanging baskets.

Care: Plant in early summer in multi-purpose compost. Water regularly (freely when hot); liquid feed fortnightly while in bloom. Straight after flowering, prune stems to half their length. Bring indoors before the first frosts; keep barely moist at 10°C (50°F) minimum. Repot in early spring.

Propagation: Grow cuttings under glass in summer; sow seeds under glass in mid-spring.

Recommended: Basic species and 'Kew Form'; also L. sessilifolius (syn. L. mascaensis), similar with yellow flowers.

Useful tip: Loss of leaves indicates that plants are too dry or too cold.

LOTUS BERTHELOTTII

This native of the Canary Islands is becoming very popular for summer bedding outdoors. In warmth and shelter plants add an exotic touch to hanging baskets and any other container that allows the slender stems, covered in masses of silvery-grey needles, to trail and show off their large scarlet blooms.

Muscari armeniacum Grape Hyacinth

MUSCARI ARMENIACUM

Grape hyacinths are so dependable that most gardeners take them for granted. The tight conical heads of blue flowers, surrounded by strap-like leaves, are always welcome in spring, and make a pretty carpet of colour under conifers and other patio shrubs. For a change, try the charming bright violet tassel hyacinth.

Plant type: Hardy perennial deciduous bulb.

Season: Flowers early to late spring.

Height: 15–30cm (6–12in).

Spread: 10–15cm (4–6in).

Positioning: Full sun. In naturalized groups 8cm (3in) apart at the edge of larger containers, the base of upright shrubs.

Care: Plant in early or mid-autumn, 8cm (3in) deep, in multi-purpose compost with extra drainage. Water regularly during growth; liquid feed every 3–4 weeks from the start of flowering. Deadhead; allow leaves to die down naturally. Divide every 3 years; replant immediately.

Propagation: Divide clumps in autumn.

Recommended: Basic species and 'Argael Album', 'Blue Spike', 'Heavenly Blue', 'Saffier'; also *M. comosum* (Tassel Hyacinth) and 'Plumosum' (syn. 'Monstrosum').

Useful tip: Shade forces vigorous leaf growth and depresses flowering.

Myosotis sylvatica (Garden) Forget-me-Not

Plant type: Hardy evergreen biennial or short-lived perennial.

Season: Flowers mid- and late spring.

Height: Up to 50cm (20in), usually less.

Spread: 15–23cm (6–9in).

Positioning: Dappled sunlight or semi-shade. 10–15cm (4–6in) apart as edging or ground cover among bulbs, in tubs and half-barrels.

Care: Plant in autumn in multi-purpose compost. Dress with general fertilizer in early spring. Water in dry weather. Discard after flowering, or deadhead; tidy old discoloured leaves. Plants usually self-seed freely.

Propagation: Transplant self-set seedlings in autumn.

Recommended: Dwarf: 'Blue Ball', 'Ultramarine', 'White Ball'. Tall: 'Bluebird', 'Blue Bouquet', 'Royal Blue'. Also M. arvensis (Wild Forget-me-Not), hardy annual or biennial.

Useful tip: Watch out for mildew on older leaves in dry weather, and spray with fungicide.

MYOSOTIS SYLVATICA

Forget-me-nots are an essential ingredient of any spring planting scheme. The plants are easily grown and intensely satisfying when the soft-leafed rosettes change into a dense carpet of tiny bright flowers, each perfectly formed and accentuated by a clear yellow eye. They are particularly effective as an edging or background to spring bulbs, but welcome anywhere in the patio.

NARCISSUS 'TÊTE-À-TÊTE'

Dwarf and species Narcissi are popular as container plants because of their compact and dainty habit, which complements pots and bowls rather than overwhelming them. Their small perfect blooms are available in shades of yellow, orange, white and even pink, and appear over a long season if varieties are selected to open in sequence.

Plant type:	Hardy perennial deciduous bulb.
Season:	Flowers late winter to mid-spring.
Height:	10–45cm (4–18in).
Spread:	10–15cm (4–6in).
Positioning:	Full sun or semi-shade. 8–15cm (3–6in) apart, alone in deep bowls and pots or grouped around shrubs in window-boxes, tubs, troughs.
Care:	Plant in early autumn, 10–15cm (4–6in) deep, in soil-based compost with extra drainage. Apply half-strength liquid fertilizer to bulbs grown alone when flowers open; repeat every 2–3 weeks while leaves are green. Dig up, dry and store bulbs until autumn, or leave in for 3 years then divide.
Propagation:	Divide clumps after the foliage dies down.
Recommended:	*N. cyclamineus* 'Tête-à-Tête'; *N. jonquilla* 'Suzy'; *N. poeticus* 'Actaea'; *N. tazetta* 'Silver Chimes'.
Useful tip:	Bulb bowls must have drainage holes at the base for outdoor cultivation.

Nerine bowdenii Nerine

Plant type: Hardy or slightly tender perennial deciduous bulb.

Season: Flowers late summer to mid-autumn.

Height: 60cm (2ft).

Spread: 15–30cm (6–12in).

Positioning: Full sun, sheltered from frost and cold winds. On their own or around a shrub in a tub or half-barrel.

Care: Plant in mid-spring or late summer, 8–10cm (3–4in) deep and 15cm (6in) apart, in soil-based compost with extra drainage. Liquid feed every 3–4 weeks while plants are in leaf. Protect in late autumn with leaves, bracken or straw; remove in spring and top-dress containers. Divide clumps when overcrowded, about every 4–5 years.

Propagation: Divide in late summer; replant immediately.

Recommended: Basic species and 'Alba', 'Mark Fenwick', 'Pink Triumph', 'Wellsii', 'Variegata'.

Useful tip: Bulbs require dividing when they push to the surface.

NERINE BOWDENII

Many nerines are slightly too tender for growing outdoors on the patio, but this species and its hybrids are hardy if grown by a warm wall with a little protection in winter. The foliage appears in spring after the bulbs have rested and then dies in summer, leaving the bright spidery blooms to appear on their own in the autumn.

Nerium oleander

NERIUM OLEANDER

This well-loved evergreen Mediterranean shrub needs very cool but frost-free winters and plenty of fresh air while in flower, making it an ideal shrub for the summer patio. A slight frost in late spring or early autumn will do no harm. Plants like to be constantly moist in summer (avoid porous clay pots), but need good drainage to prevent waterlogging.

Plant type: Slightly tender perennial evergreen shrub.

Season: Flowers early summer to mid-autumn; foliage all year.

Height: Up to 1.8m (6ft).

Spread: 90cm–1.2m (3–4ft).

Positioning: Full sun, in warmth. In plastic or wooden tubs and half-barrels.

Care: Plant in late spring in multi-purpose compost with extra drainage. Water copiously in dry weather; liquid feed fortnightly while in flower. After flowering, shorten side-shoots to about 8cm (3in). Bring indoors in early autumn, overwinter at 7°C (45°F) minimum; keep dry for a few weeks. Top-dress in spring.

Propagation: Grow cuttings under glass in summer.

Recommended: Basic species, and cultivars, some difficult: try 'Clare', 'Géant des Batailles', 'Luteum Plenum', 'Peach Blossom', 'Variegatum'.

Useful tip: All parts of the plant are poisonous: wear gloves when pruning.

Nicotiana alata
Tobacco Plant, Flowering Tobacco

Plant type: Tender perennial, usually grown as a half-hardy annual.

Season: Flowers early summer to mid-autumn.

Height: 25–90cm (10in–3ft).

Spread: 25–45cm (10–18in).

Positioning: Full sun or very light shade. 15–23cm (6–9in) apart as bedding in pots, troughs, tubs.

Care: Plant after the last frosts in multi-purpose compost; water in well. Protect from slugs while young. Water in dry weather; feed occasionally with high-potash liquid fertilizer. Stake tall varieties. Discard after flowering.

Propagation: Surface-sow seeds under glass in early or mid-spring.

Recommended: Flowers of 'Crimson Bedder', 'Nikki Mixed', 'VIP' remain open all day; 'Lime Green'; 'Affinis' (syn. N. alata grandiflora), tall, white and fragrant; N. glauca, hardy blue-leafed shrub, yellow flowers.

Useful tip: Watch out for greenfly, and spray heavy infestations.

NICOTIANA ALATA 'DOMINO'

The varieties of flowering tobacco that are noted for their glorious perfume tend to be tall and need support when grown in containers. Modern hybrids are shorter, with bright flowers that remain open all day, but usually lack scent. A massed display of either kind is dramatically colourful all summer. (syns N affinis, N. × sanderae.)

Osteospermum hybrids Osteospermum

OSTEOSPERMUM 'LADY LEITRIM'

In recent years numerous beautiful hybrids have been developed from the basic South African species, and have become popular for summer bedding: hot bright sunshine guarantees a luxuriant display all season. They are on the borderline of hardiness, and may be kept from year to year if they are overwintered in a cool greenhouse.

Plant type: Slightly tender perennials, usually grown as half-hardy annuals.

Season: Flowers early summer to mid-autumn.

Height: Up to 60cm (2ft).

Spread: 30–45cm (12–18in).

Positioning: Full sun, in shelter. In threes in large pots; as edging around a tub or larger container.

Care: Plant after the last frosts, 38cm (15in) apart, in soil-based compost with added drainage. Water freely until late summer, then reduce quantities; liquid feed every 4 weeks. Take cuttings in summer. Discard plants after flowering, or bring under cool glass in autumn; keep above 4°C (40°F). Repot in spring.

Propagation: Grow cuttings in heat in spring or summer.

Recommended: 'Blue Streak', 'Silver Sparkler', 'Tresco Purple', 'Buttermilk', 'Pink Whirls'; also shrubby *O. ecklonis* and 'Prostratum'.

Useful tip: Plants kept above 10°C (50°F) in full sun may flower all winter.

Pelargonium peltatum Ivy(-leafed) Geranium

Plant type: Tender perennial evergreen trailing shrub.

Season: Early summer to mid-autumn.

Height: 15cm (6in).

Spread: Trails to 90cm (3ft).

Positioning: Full sun or very light shade. As bedding in window-boxes, wall pots, hanging baskets; edging in tubs.

Care: Plant after the last frosts in soil-based compost with extra drainage. Water freely in dry weather; liquid feed with high-potash fertilizer every 3–4 weeks. Deadhead; remove yellow leaves; Pinch shoot tips that extend too far. Bring indoors in autumn and keep barely moist at 7°C (45°F) minimum. Repot in early spring and cut back hard.

Propagation: Grow cuttings under glass in mid- to late summer.

Recommended: Variety: 'Harlequin'. Zonal Pelargonium: 'Happy Thoughts'. Regal types: 'Grand Slam', 'Pompeii'.

Useful tip: Sow seeds under glass in mid- to late winter.

PELARGONIUM PELTATUM VAR.

This is the classic trailing plant for summer bedding, not just in wall pots and hanging baskets – which a few plants can turn into balls of bright colour – but also nearer the ground, cascading from a strawberry tower or edging a tub of upright zonal geraniums. They are easily kept from one year to the next, and provide dependable colour in hot dry conditions.

Petunia Petunia

PETUNIA 'SURFINIA'

Petunias have always been popular bedding plants, but the advent of more prolific, and increasingly weatherproof, trailing varieties has made them the supreme choice for flamboyant summer containers. Plants revel in hot weather, and often disappear beneath showy trumpets in a huge range of bright colours.

Plant type: Tender perennial, usually grown as a half-hardy annual.

Season: Flowers early summer to early autumn.

Height: 15–45cm (6–18in).

Spread: 20–30cm (8–12in), trailers to 90cm (3ft) or more.

Positioning: Full sun. 23–30cm (9–12in) apart, as edging in tubs, trailers in baskets, window-boxes; bedding.

Care: Plant after the last frosts in multi-purpose compost. Water freely in dry weather; while flowering, liquid feed with high-potash fertilizer. Deadhead; trim back leggy stems. After flowering discard or bring indoors and keep just moist at 4°C (40°F) minimum. In early spring repot and cut back hard.

Propagation: Grow cuttings under glass in spring.

Recommended: Trailers: 'Purple wave', 'Surfinia'. Multiflora: 'Celebrity'. Grandiflora: 'Merlin'.

Useful tip: For bushy growth, pinch out growing tips 2–3 times while plants are small.

Polystichum setiferum Soft-shield fern

Plant type: Hardy perennial deciduous fern.

Season: Foliage all year.

Height: Up to 1.2m (4ft).

Spread: 90cm (3ft).

Positioning: Light or semi-shade, sheltered from drying winds. As foliage plants in medium-size pots, troughs; dwarf forms in shallow pots, window-boxes.

Care: Plant in spring or early summer in soil-based compost; mulch with gravel or bark. Water well in dry weather; liquid feed every 4–6 weeks. In spring cut off old fronds with scissors, and repot or top-dress.

Propagation: Divide crowns in spring or surface-sow ripe spores under glass in autumn.

Recommended: Basic species and many ornamental variations; also *Adiantum pedatum*, *Dryopteris erythrosora*, *Polypodium vulgare*.

Useful tip: Check specific ferns before planting: some prefer dry conditions and a few need acid compost.

POLYSTICHUM SETIFERUM

One of the most beautiful and elegant ferns, this is almost evergreen – the old fronds only collapse in spring as new fresh green leaves unfurl. Many other choice ferns will also grow happily in containers, some in full sun although most revel in cool moist shade. They all make good companions for flowering plants.

Pieris Pieris

PIERIS FORMOSA VAR. FORRESTII

This woodland species enjoys warmth, shelter and light shade and, given these conditions, the neat slow-growing bushes develop spectacular spring colours as white, pink or red buds open into long sprays of white bell-shaped flowers. Many varieties produce bright red or pink new shoots at the same time.

Plant type: Hardy perennial evergreen shrub.

Season: Flowers and young red foliage early to late spring.

Height: 1.5–1.8m (5–6ft).

Spread: 1.2–1.5m (4–5ft).

Positioning: Light or dappled shade, sheltered from cold winds. As a specimen shrub in tubs and half-barrels.

Care: Plant in spring in ericaceous (lime-free) compost. Water freely with rainwater in dry weather; feed with rhododendron fertilizer after flowering. Insulate containers with bubble plastic over winter. Remove frost-damaged shoots in late spring, shorten vigorous stems. Top-dress in late winter.

Propagation: Grow cuttings under glass in summer.

Recommended: P. formosa var. forrestii 'Jermyns', 'Wakehurst'; P. japonica 'Blush', 'Christmas Cheer', 'Flamingo', 'Purity'; P. 'Forest Flame', 'Flaming Silver'.

Useful tip: Some forms bloom from late winter in a warm sheltered place.

Pittosporum tobira Japanese Pittosporum, Mock Orange

Plant type: Hardy or slightly tender perennial evergreen shrub.

Season: Flowers in late spring; foliage all year.

Height: 3m (10ft).

Spread: Up to 1.8m (6ft).

Positioning: Full sun or light shade, in a warm spot sheltered from frost and cold winds. In a large pot or tub.

Care: Plant in late spring in soil-based compost with extra drainage. Water freely in dry weather. Prune new shoots by up to one-third after flowering. In cold gardens move pots under glass in autumn, or insulate them and protect foliage with fleece. Repot or top-dress in mid-spring.

Propagation: Grow cuttings under glass in summer.

Recommended: Basic species and 'Nanum', 'Variegatum'; also P. tenuifolium and 'Irene Patterson', 'Silver Queen', 'Tom Thumb'; P. 'Garnettii'.

Useful tip: Plants are clipped as topiary in some coastal gardens.

PITTOSPORUM TOBIRA 'NANUM'

These handsome shrubs are ideal for containers because their dense and distinctive evergreen foliage makes them perfect structural plants to give height and volume to patio plantings. They are only just hardy in mild gardens, and elsewhere benefit from winter protection.

Primula × pruhonicensis

PRIMULA × PRUHONICENSIS

Many Primulas grow contentedly in patio containers, but perhaps the most popular are the many polyanthus hybrids, all of which are derived from the wild primrose or cowslip. They are usually treated as bedding, but may be grown as permanent ground cover under large shrubs. (syn. *P. × polyantha*.)

Plant type: Hardy evergreen perennial.

Season: Flowers early to late spring.

Height: 23–30cm (9–12in).

Spread: 20–23cm (8–9in).

Positioning: Full sun or semi-shade. 20cm (8in) apart as permanent plants or bedding in pots, tubs and window-boxes.

Care: Plant in multi-purpose compost in very early spring or mid-autumn. Water in dry weather. Protect against slugs. Deadhead unless seeds are wanted. After flowering lift bedding plants, divide and replant in a shady border. Top-dress other plants in late winter; divide every 3–4 years.

Propagation: Divide after flowering; sow seeds in a frame in early summer.

Recommended: 'Crescendo' and 'Rainbow' mixtures; 'Pacific Giants'; 'Chartreuse', 'Gold Lace'; *P. denticulata*, *P. auricula* for sinks, strawberry pots.

Useful tip: Deter birds with short twigs or black cotton when buds appear.

Rhododendron Rhododendron, Azalea

Plant type: Hardy perennial evergreen or deciduous shrub.

Season: Flowers early spring to early summer.

Height: Up to 1.8m (6ft).

Spread: 1.2–1.8m (4–6ft).

Positioning: Dappled sunlight or semi-shade, sheltered from winds. In tubs and half-barrels.

Care: Plant deciduous kinds in autumn and winter, evergreens in spring, in lime-free compost with extra drainage. Water in dry weather with rainwater; liquid feed monthly from spring to autumn. Deadhead to make way for new shoots. Prune lightly if necessary in winter. Top-dress in spring.

Propagation: Layer in autumn or spring.

Recommended: Dwarf rhododendrons: 'Blue Tit', 'Pink Drift'; R. yakushimanum hybrids 'Doc', 'Vintage Rose' 'Percy Whiteman'. Azaleas: Kaempferi Hybrid 'Fedora'; Vuyk Hybrid 'Blue Danube'.

Useful tip: Treat yellowing leaves with sequestered iron and rainwater.

RHODODENDRON YAKUSHIMANUM 'DOC'

Many gardeners cannot grow rhododendrons because their soil is too alkaline, but containers filled with lime-free compost, and watering with rainwater, provide the perfect conditions. Most varieties prefer some shade to prevent their flowers scorching, but in the north full sun is advisable to ripen new stems.

Rosa Patio Rose

ROSA 'SHINE ON'

Most roses, even ramblers and climbers, can be grown in containers, but the most successful are the dwarf cluster-flowered varieties, popularly known as patio roses, and their tiny cousins, the miniature roses. The neat compact bushes resemble larger types and need similar treatment, but have more charm and impact as most of them are very free-flowering with dense foliage.

Plant type:	Hardy perennial deciduous shrub.
Season:	Flowers early summer to early autumn.
Height:	23–45cm (9–18in).
Spread:	Up to 45cm (18in).
Positioning:	Full sun. 30–38cm (12–15in) apart in groups, or as specimens, in pots and tubs at least 30cm (12in) deep.
Care:	Plant bare-root roses from early winter to early spring, container ones at any time, in multi-purpose compost with extra drainage. Water regularly in dry weather. Apply rose fertilizer in spring, mid-summer. Trim with scissors or secateurs in late winter or early spring; remove dead or weak growth. In spring repot or top-dress with decayed manure mixed with fresh compost.
Propagation:	Grow cuttings under glass in early autumn.
Recommended:	Miniature: 'Angela Rippon', 'Red Ace'. Patio: 'Anna Ford'.
Useful tip:	Make sure compost in plastic containers is very well-drained.

Scaevola Fan Flower

Plant type: Tender perennial prostrate or trailing evergreen shrub.

Season: Flowers early summer to mid-autumn.

Height: Up to 30cm (12in).

Spread: 60–75cm (24–30in).

Positioning: Full sun, sheltered from cold winds. As trailers in hanging baskets and window-boxes; bedding in tubs and larger containers.

Care: Plant after the last frosts in soil-based compost. Pinch the tips of young plants once or twice. Water in dry weather; liquid feed with high-potash fertilizer every 3–4 weeks. Shorten long bare stems. Discard after flowering, or bring under glass in autumn and keep just moist at 4°C (40°F) minimum. Repot and trim to shape in spring.

Propagation: Grow cuttings under glass in summer.

Recommended: Many *S. aemula* hybrids include 'Blue Fan', 'Blue Wonder', 'Petite', 'Alba'; also *S. crassifolia*.

Useful tip: Avoid over-watering, but ensure plants do not dry out completely.

SCAEVOLA AEMULA

These fascinating plants are natives of Australia, where they grow in bright sunlight and very often in dry sand. Grown for years as conservatory plants, they are now popular summer bedding plants. Their curious one-sided blue, mauve or white blooms open prolifically all summer.

SEMPERVIVUM ARACHNOIDEUM SSP. TOMENTOSUM

These succulents are intriguing because of the beautiful symmetry of their densely packed leaf rosettes, and the ability of plants to thrive and flower apparently on nothing. They enjoy hot dry spots – some forms even resent winter rains – and in summer suddenly produce thick leafy stems capped with pretty star-like blooms.

Plant type: Hardy perennial evergreen succulent.

Season: Flowers early and mid-summer; foliage all year.

Height: 8–15cm (3–6in).

Spread: Up to 45cm (18in).

Positioning: Full sun and exposure. As edging in pots and troughs; specimens in alpine sinks.

Care: Plant in autumn or spring in soil-based compost with added grit and extra drainage; set lowest leaves at soil level and mulch with grit or gravel. Water now and then in very dry weather. Deadhead; remove exhausted rosettes after flowering. Feed in spring with slow-release pellets.

Propagation: Detach young rooted offsets at any time.

Recommended: *S. arachnoideum* and ssp. *tomentosum*, 'Clairchen'; *S. tectorum* 'Red Flush'; 'Sunset'; many coloured hybrids like 'Othello', 'Pekinese', 'Commander Hay'.

Useful tip: Flowering rosettes die and leave rooted offsets on runners.

Senecio cineraria Dusty Miller

SENECIO CINERARIA 'CIRRUS'

Plant type: Hardy or slightly tender perennial evergreen shrub, often grown as a half-hardy annual.

Season: Foliage all year.

Height: 20–45cm (8–18in).

Spread: 15–30cm (6–12in).

Positioning: Full sun in warmth. 15–25cm (6–10in) apart as edging or in groups, in pots, tubs and window-boxes.

Care: Plant in late spring in soil-based compost with extra drainage. Water regularly in dry weather; avoid water-logging. In early and mid-summer liquid feed with high-potash fertilizer. Remove flowers at bud stage. Discard plants after flowering, or pot up and keep frost-free and barely moist under glass. Repot in early spring; take cuttings.

Propagation: Grow cuttings under glass in spring or summer.

Recommended: 'Silver Dust', 'Alice', 'White Diamond'; also hardy *S. greyi* (now *Brachyglottis*) and 'Sunshine'.

Useful tip: Protect from slugs and snails.

Varieties of this familiar bedding plant range from miniature to tall. The leaves of some kinds are finely cut and lacy, others are broad and oval, but all are covered in silvery-white hairs that seem to shine in the sun. Plants can survive as perennials if winters are dry as dampness, not frost, is their main enemy. (syns *S. maritimus*, *Cineraria maritima*.)

Solenostemon hybrids Flame Nettle, Coleus

SOLENOSTEMON 'SURPRISE'

Coleus varieties come in a dazzling range of leaf shades and patterns and are often more colourful than many flowering plants. Their shapes vary almost as extravagantly as their foliage, with fringed, lacy, ruffled and nettle-like forms sometimes occurring in a single seed mixture. Although they are perennials, the best plants are grown from cuttings taken each year. (syn. *Coleus blumei*.)

Plant type: Tender perennial evergreen shrub, often grown as a half-hardy annual.

Season: Foliage all year.

Height: 15–45cm (6–18in).

Spread: 15–38cm (6–15in).

Positioning: Full sun (for colour) or light shade, sheltered from cold winds. As bedding or specimens, in pots, tubs and window-boxes.

Care: Plant after last frosts in soil-based compost. In dry weather water well. Liquid feed with high-potash fertilizer from mid-summer. Pinch tips of shoots; support tall varieties with twiggy sticks. Remove buds while small. Discard old plants. Take cuttings in late summer.

Propagation: Grow cuttings under glass in spring and summer; surface sow seeds under glass in late winter.

Recommended: Seed mixtures 'Sabre', 'Wizard', 'Red Velvet'; also 'Paisley Shawl'.

Useful tip: For spring cuttings, pot up in autumn, and keep frost-free and just moist indoors.

Thunbergia alata Black-eyed Susan

Plant type: Tender perennial climber, usually grown as a half-hardy annual.

Season: Flowers early summer to early autumn.

Height: 1.5–3m (5–10ft).

Spread: 45–60cm (18–24in).

Positioning: Full sun, sheltered from winds. Climbing on supports in large pots and tubs; trailing in window-boxes, hanging baskets.

Care: Plant after the last frosts in soil-based compost. Water freely in dry weather; liquid feed with high-potash fertilizer every 2–3 weeks while in flower. Support climbers on a pyramid of canes and strings or trellis. After flowering, discard or move indoors and keep barely moist and frost-free. Repot and cut back in spring.

Propagation: Sow seeds under glass in early spring.

Recommended: Basic species, often in a mixture, and 'Susie'; also *T. erecta* and 'Alba'; *T. mysorensis*.

Useful tip: Grow 3 plants on a cane tripod, 30–38cm (12–15in) apart, in a tub of bedding.

THUNBERGIA ALATA 'SUNDANCE'

These slender climbers are little trouble to grow, provided they are kept warm and out of draughts. In a sheltered corner of the patio, they will flower for weeks on end. Mixed seedlings produce orange, yellow and white 5cm (2in) flowers, often with an intriguingly dark eye, and make an arresting combination against the lush foliage.

THYMUS VULGARIS

Herbs of all kinds enjoy pot culture on a patio, where they are readily accessible for use. With hundreds of attractive species and varieties available, thyme is possibly the best one for imaginative container schemes. Variegated types, in particular, blend usefulness with decorative foliage and flowers.

Plant type: Hardy perennial aromatic evergreen shrub.

Season: Flowers mid- and late summer; foliage all year.

Height: 30cm (12in).

Spread: 30–45cm (12–18in).

Positioning: Full sun. With other herbs in a tub, trough or window-box; different kinds in a strawberry tower.

Care: Plant in spring or autumn in soil-based compost with extra drainage and added grit; mulch with grit. Water regularly in dry weather. Trim in mid-summer, or clip to shape after blooms fade, again in autumn. In spring, feed with slow-release pellets or top-dress, divide and repot every 2–3 years.

Propagation: Grow cuttings in a frame in summer.

Recommended: T. x citriodorus 'Aureus'; T. herba-barona; T. serpyllum coccineus, 'Pink Chintz'; T. vulgaris aureus, 'Silver Posie'.

Useful tip: Turn pots and towers occasionally to expose all sides to full sun.

Plant type: Hardy or slightly tender perennial evergreen palm.

Season: Foliage all year.

Height: 1.8–3m (6–10ft).

Spread: 1.8m (6ft) or more.

Positioning: Light or semi-shade, in warmth sheltered from frost and cold winds. As a specimen in a tub or half-barrel.

Care: Plant in spring in soil-based compost with added grit and extra drainage. Water freely in spring and summer, otherwise moderately. In winter bring small plants under cover, keep above 4°C (40°F); bring in mature plants or leave outside in mild gardens: insulate pots with bubble plastic. In spring feed with slow-release pellets and repot or top-dress every 4–5 years.

Propagation: Sow seeds under glass in spring.

Recommended: Basic species and *T. wagnerianus*; in a warm summer, try *Chamaerops humilis*.

Useful tip: Propagate new plants from suckers on the base of the parent.

TRACHYCARPUS FORTUNEI

Palms add flair and tropical exuberance to a patio, and survive for many years in large containers. They enjoy standing outdoors in summer, but winter protection is advisable as most plants resent temperatures below 13°C (55°F).

Tropaeolum majus Nasturtium

TROPAEOLUM MAJUS 'EMPRESS OF INDIA'

Nasturtiums are old favourites with large flowers, in rich vibrant shades, supported by handsome foliage which is particularly attractive when variegated. They are a valuable stand-by for adding last-minute colour to patio plantings, as seeds can be pushed into the compost at any time up to mid-summer and resulting plants will grow very quickly.

Plant type: Hardy or slightly tender annual.

Season: Flowers early summer to early autumn.

Height: 30cm (12in) or 2.4m (8ft).

Spread: Up to 60cm (24in).

Positioning: Full sun or light shade. Dwarf bedding 20cm (8in) apart as edging in pots, tubs; climbers on trellis in tubs or trailing in window-boxes and hanging baskets.

Care: Plant in multi-purpose compost in late spring. Water often in dry weather; liquid feed at half-strength every 2 weeks while flowering. Support climbers on trellis or large shrubs. Watch out for blackfly, slugs and caterpillars. Discard after flowering.

Propagation: Sow under glass in late winter or early spring, or in situ in mid-spring.

Recommended: Climbers: 'Tall Mixed Hybrids'. Trailing: climbing varieties. Dwarf: 'Peach Melba', 'Tom Thumb'.

Useful tip: Remove seeds and pinch out growing tips if flowering flags.

Plant type:	Hardy perennial deciduous bulb.
Season:	Flowers late winter to early summer.
Height:	15–30in (6–12in).
Spread:	10–20cm (4–8in).
Positioning:	Full sun, sheltered from cold winds. As bedding, 10–15cm (4–6in) apart, in pots and bowls; in groups of 4–5 around shrubs in tubs, half-barrels.
Care:	Plant in late autumn and early winter, 10cm (4in) deep, in multi-purpose compost with extra drainage. Water regularly in spring and summer; liquid feed every 2–3 weeks from bud formation until leaves fade. Deadhead. In late summer, dig up bulbs, dry and store; or leave, top-dress in late winter and divide every 4–5 years.
Propagation:	Remove small offsets after leaves die down; replant in autumn.
Recommended:	*T. fosteriana* 'Madame Lefeber'; *T. greigii*; *T. kaufmanniana* 'Giuseppe Verde'.
Useful tip:	Grow with blue forget-me-nots (*Myosotis*).

TULIPA GREIGII 'MARY ANN'

The short-stemmed Botanical and Species tulips are best for containers, because they are relatively compact, tough and long-lasting, and tolerate being left undisturbed for several years. Their flowering season stretches from late winter to early spring, depending on the variety. Plant generously and remember to build up the bulbs for the next year by feeding until the foliage dies down naturally.

Verbena Verbena

VERBENA 'LINDA'

With their bright colours and exuberant growth, modern verbena hybrids are essential summer ingredients of hanging baskets, window-boxes and other patio containers in full sun. Once established, plants are irrepressible and flower continuously until the frosts. They can be easily kept from one year to the next in a cool greenhouse.

Plant type:	Tender perennial evergreen, often grown as a half-hardy annual.
Season:	Flowers early summer to mid-autumn.
Height:	15–45cm (6–12in).
Spread:	30–50cm (12–20in).
Positioning:	Full sun. 30cm (12in) apart, as trailers in hanging baskets and window-boxes, edging for pots and tubs.
Care:	Plant in multi-purpose compost after last frosts. Water regularly in dry weather; liquid feed with high-potash fertilizer every 2–3 weeks. Pinch growing tips of young plants several times; dead-head regularly. After flowering discard, or pot up and keep barely moist under glass at 4°C (40°F) minimum.
Propagation:	Sow under glass in early spring.
Recommended:	Many V. × hybrida seed mixtures include 'Olympia', 'Peaches and Cream', 'Quartz', and single colours like 'Amethyst', 'Blaze', 'Silver Anne'.
Useful tip:	Germination may be slow and erratic.

Vinca minor Lesser Periwinkle

Plant type: Hardy perennial evergreen creeping subshrub.

Season: Flowers mid- to late spring, intermittently until early autumn; foliage all year.

Height: 30cm (12in).

Spread: Up to 1.8m (6ft); limited by pot size.

Positioning: Full sun or shade. As ground cover, edging, 23–30cm (9–12in) apart, in larger tubs and half-barrels.

Care: Plant in autumn or spring in multi-purpose compost; set plants to their previous depth. Water in dry weather. Cut to the ground in autumn after flowering or in late winter. Top-dress in spring or feed with slow-release pellets. Divide stems every few years.

Propagation: Divide plants in autumn or spring.

Recommended: Basic species and 'Burgundy', 'Gertrude Jekyll', 'Multiplex', variegated forms.

Useful tip: Many lovely forms of tender *Vinca rosea* (now *Catharanthus roseus*), can be grown in warm positions.

VINCA MINOR 'GERTRUDE JEKYLL'

There are more than a dozen lovely types of this weatherproof cottage garden plant, all slightly invasive in good soil and therefore ideal for containers where their growth will be confined. With their strong performance in shade and as ground cover, they are ideal for less favoured corners of a patio.

Viola Viola, Pansy

VIOLA ULTIMA SERIES

With careful selection it is possible to have different types of viola and pansy in flower at any time. Only in the depths of winter does their energy flag a little, but true winter-flowering strains spring to life again after a few days of sun. Plant the various kinds liberally and try some of the less well-known species, which tend to revel in cool shade.

Plant type: Hardy evergreen perennial, usually grown as a half-hardy annual or hardy biennial.

Season: Flowers for 4–6 months, any time.

Height: 10–23cm (4–9in).

Spread: Up to 30cm (12in).

Positioning: Full sun or semi-shade. 15cm (6in) apart as seasonal bedding; Violas in alpine sinks, window-boxes, pots; Pansies in any container especially as edging.

Care: Plant in multi-purpose compost in spring or autumn. Water in dry weather; liquid feed with high potash fertilizer every 2–3 weeks in spring, summer. Deadhead. Shorten leggy stems occasionally. Divide or discard after flowering.

Propagation: Divide in autumn or spring.

Recommended: Summer Pansies: 'Swiss Giants', 'Azure Blue'. Winter Pansies: 'Universal', 'Premiere'. Violas: 'Arkwright Ruby', 'Chantreyland'.

Useful tip: Watch out for aphids in summer.